Colores: verde
Colors: Green

D1377748

Esther Sarfatti

Rourke
Publishing LLC
Vero Beach, Florida 32964

www.rourkepublishing.com

PHOTO CREDITS: © Miroslav Ferkuniak: title page; © Viorika Prikhodko: page 3; © Don Bayley: page 5; © Olga Shelego: page 9; © Nico Smit: page 11; © Robert Churchill: page 17; © Denise Bentley: page 21; © Christine Balderas, Denis Sauvageau, Robert Dodge: page 23.

Editor: Robert Stengard-Olliges

Cover design by Nicola Stratford, bdpublishing.com

Library of Congress Cataloging-in-Publication Data

Sarfatti, Esther.
   Colors : green / Esther Sarfatti.
      p. cm. -- (Concepts)
   ISBN 978-1-60044-518-7 (Hardcover)
   ISBN 978-1-60044-659-7 (Softcover)
   1. Colors--Juvenile literature. 2. Green--Juvenile literature. I. Title.
   QC495.5.S356 2008
   535.6--dc22
                              2007014028

Printed in the USA

CG/CG

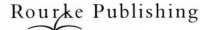

Rourke Publishing

www.rourkepublishing.com – rourke@rourkepublishing.com
Post Office Box 3328, Vero Beach, FL 32964

Esta página es verde.
This page is green.

El verde es mi color favorito.

Green is my favorite color.

Me gustan los árboles verdes.

I like green trees.

Me gustan las uvas verdes.

I like green grapes.

Me gustan las ranas verdes.

I like green frogs.

Me gustan las
serpientes verdes.

I like green snakes.

13

Me gustan los
lagartos verdes.

I like green lizards.

15

Me gustan las
sandías verdes.

I like green watermelons.

Me gusta la hierba verde.

I like green grass.

Me gustan los
tréboles verdes.

I like green clovers.

Hay muchas cosas verdes.
¿Te gusta el verde también?

So many things are green.
Do you like green, too?

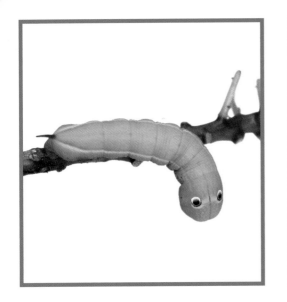

Índice

Index

Lecturas adicionales / Further Reading

Anderson, Moira. *Finding Colors: Green*. Heinemann, 2005.
Schuette, Sarah L. *Green: Seeing Green All Around Us*.
  Capstone Press, 2006.

Páginas Web recomendadas / Recommended Websites

www.enchantedlearning.com/colors/green.shtml

Acerca de la autora / About the Author

Esther Sarfatti lleva más de 15 años trabajando con libros infantiles como editora y traductora. Ésta es su primera serie como autora. Nacida en Brooklyn, Nueva York, donde creció en una familia trilingüe, Esther vive actualmente en Madrid, España, con su esposo y su hijo.

Esther Sarfatti has worked with children's books for over 15 years as an editor and translator. This is her first series as an author. Born in Brooklyn, New York, and brought up in a trilingual home, Esther currently lives with her husband and son in Madrid, Spain.